Conte

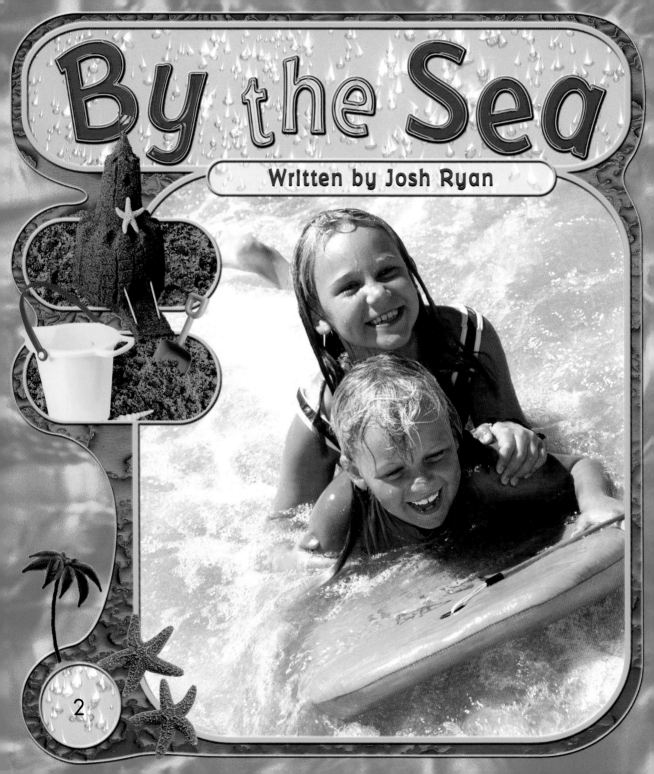

By the Sea

Written by Josh Ryan

We bring beach balls and boogie boards.
We bring buckets and spades.
We bring sunhats and sunscreen.

We make sandcastles and look for shells.
We ride the waves
on our boogie boards.

Shells

Sometimes, when the tide is out, we look for crabs and starfish in the tide pools.

Crabs and starfish share their home with sea anemones, sea snails, and little fish.

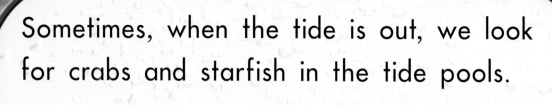

Sea snail

Sea anemones

We are always careful
not to hurt anything.
We never take anything away.

Hermit crab

Starfish

Crab

5

Sometimes, when the tide is in,
we put on masks and snorkels.
We dive under the water.

We see lots of fish.
They swim in big schools
and dart in and out
of the rocks and seaweed.

A day by the sea is fun!

Song ♪ of the Sea

Flip, flap, flip, flop.
Lip, lap, slip, slop.

Waves break,
pebbles clatter.
Seagulls call,
children chatter.

8

Make an Underwater Viewer

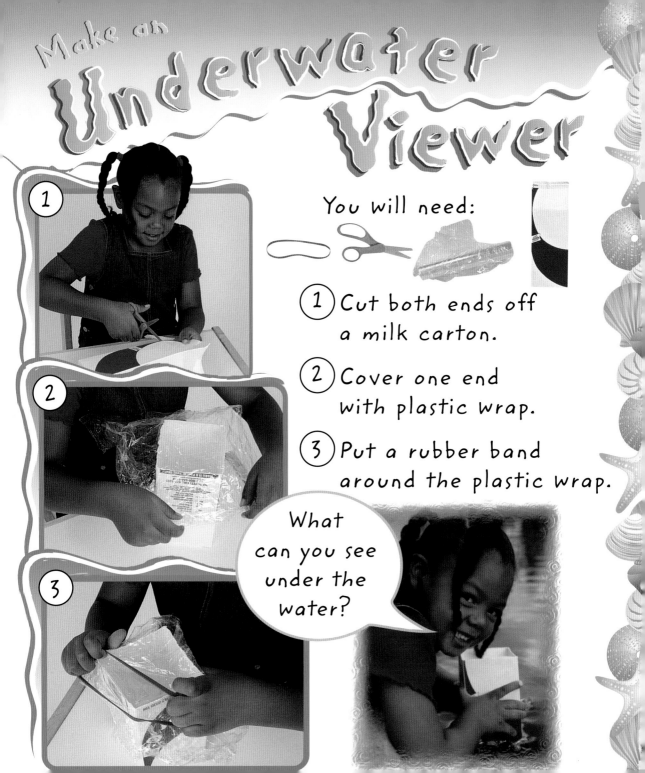

You will need:

1 Cut both ends off a milk carton.

2 Cover one end with plastic wrap.

3 Put a rubber band around the plastic wrap.

What can you see under the water?

Seaside

seagull

seabed

What can you find
that begins with
the word **sea**?

sea star

seaweed

sea pen

sea lion

sea egg

10

Splish, splash, splosh, splish,
fins fan, tails swish.

Soft sounds
the sea brings.
Evening comes,
the seaside sings.

Use the big picture to help you find
ten things that begin with the word **sea**.

```
s e a s h e l l s s
e b f e x g c i e e
a s e a s l u g a a
s p h g s v q n a w
t n a u h t x s n e
a e y l q e r l e e
r p w l r j m k m d
n a t s e a l i o n
s e a e g g h i n l
b s e a h o r s e z
```

Surprises

sea turtle

sea horse

sea anemone

sea snail

11

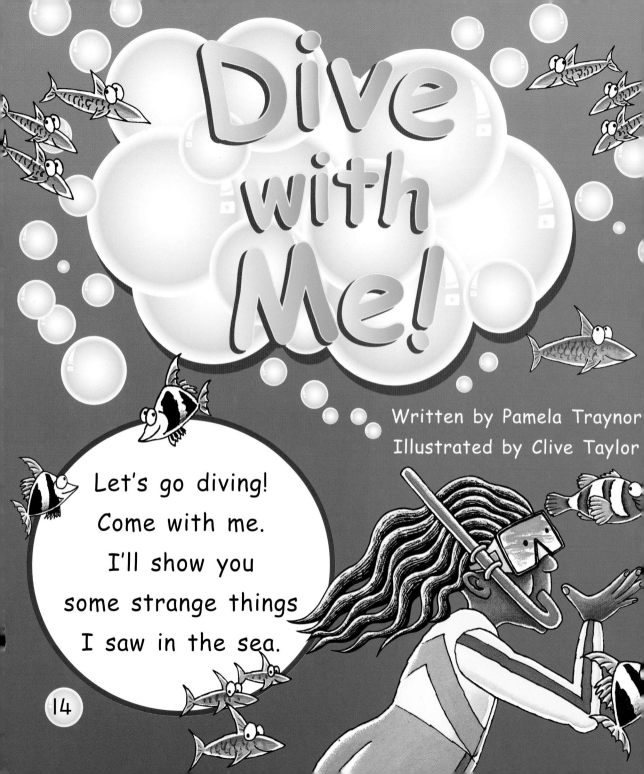

Dive with Me!

Written by Pamela Traynor
Illustrated by Clive Taylor

Let's go diving!
Come with me.
I'll show you
some strange things
I saw in the sea.

King of the Castle

Written by Josh Ryan Illustrated by Christen Stewart

Lucy and Leo went to the beach
with Grandma and Grandpa.

Lucy, Leo, and Grandpa
began to work on the castle.

20

21

And here are some feathers for the turrets.

Here are some shells for the castle.

Grandma helped, too.
Grandma, Grandpa, and the children
worked and worked
and worked.

After a while, Grandma
got their picnic lunch ready.

Lucy stopped working on the castle.
Leo stopped working on the castle.

But Grandpa didn't stop
working on the castle.
He made a big stone wall.
He made slits for windows.
He made towers and arches.

25

Captain Skilly's Trawler

Written and Illustrated by Martin Bailey

Captain Skilly was a fisherman.
Every day, he went to sea
in his fishing boat.
Every day, he took a sandwich
and some cake for his lunch.

At lunchtime, Captain Skilly
sat on the deck and ate his lunch.
The seagulls always came to help
Captain Skilly eat his lunch.

When the sun began to go down,
Captain Skilly would start the motor
and chug-chug-chug back to town.
He always got home before it was dark.

But, one day, Captain Skilly
couldn't get the motor to go.
The sun was going down.
The wind was blowing hard.
The waves were getting big.

Captain Skilly looked at his charts.
"What can I do?" he said.
"It's a long way back to town."

Just then,
a flock of seagulls flew by.
One big seagull flew down
and landed on the rope.

It took
the rope
in its beak
and flew
up, up, up.

The other seagulls took the rope in their beaks.
The boat rocked in the waves.
The seagulls held
onto the rope
and pulled.

Slowly,
the seagulls
pulled Captain
Skilly's boat
back to town.

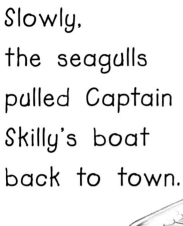

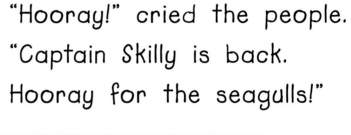

"Hooray!" cried the people.
"Captain Skilly is back.
Hooray for the seagulls!"

Now, when Captain Skilly sits on the deck to eat his lunch, he brings an extra piece of cake and some bread for his friends the seagulls!

Mr. Sun

and

Mr. Sea

A Traditional Tale | Illustrated by Elliot Cowan

Long ago, the sun lived
in a house by the sea.

The sun and the sea
were good friends.

37

One day, the sun said,

"Mr. Sea, I come to see you every day.

Why don't you come to my house

to see me?"

"I would like to come, Mr. Sun," said Mr. Sea, "but I could not leave my children on their own."

"Then bring your children with you," said Mr. Sun.

"All right, Mr. Sun," said Mr. Sea. "We'll come tomorrow."

The next day,
there was a tap on the door.
"Yoo-hoo, Mr. Sun,"
called a voice.
"We're here."

40

Mr. Sun opened the door.
"Hello, Mr. Sea. Please come in."

"I hope you have room for us,
Mr. Sun," said his friend.

"There is lots of room,"
said Mr. Sun. "Come in. Come in."

41

Mr. Sea went into Mr. Sun's house.
"Come along, children," he called.

So in went his children.
There were starfish, crabs,
seahorses, and shrimps.

Soon the sea
covered the floor.

"Hello, hello," said Mr. Sun.
"I'm so pleased you've come to see me."

43

Next came lots of little fish.

"Are you sure there is room, Mr. Sun?" asked Mr. Sea.

"Oh, yes, my friend, there is lots of room," said Mr. Sun.

So the sea kept coming in.
"How many children does
Mr. Sea have?" thought Mr. Sun.

45

Mr. Sun looked outside.
He saw sharks, seals, dolphins,
and whales waiting to come in.

46

"I must do something," he cried.
The sea was filling up his house,
so Mr. Sun climbed up onto the roof.

47

Still the sea kept coming in.

Mr. Sun climbed up onto his chimney,
but the sea got higher and higher.

"There's only one thing I can do,"
cried Mr. Sun, and he jumped
as high as he could,
up, up, up into the sky.

The sun lives
in the sky now.
But if you look out to sea
at sunrise or at sunset,
you will see Mr. Sun
talking to Mr. Sea.
Mr. Sun and Mr. Sea
are still good friends!

51

Letters That Go Together

ch children   **cl** clatter

fl flip, flap   **spl** splish, splash

Sounds I Know

-ai mail   **-ay** ray

-ale whale   **-ei** sleigh

Endings I Know

-ed   call, called

cry, cried

stop, stopped

Words I Know

always	children	let's	stopped
back	could	made	there's
bring	cried	make	took
called	friends	please	when